MY VEHICLE IS A "LEMON" NOW WHAT?

SHALEV AMAR, ESQ.

Jacobs & Whitehall
21750 Hardy Oak Blvd
Suite 104 – 51700
San Antonio, Texas 78258
(888) 570-7338
www.jacobsandwhitehall.com

Ordering Information:

Quantity sales. Special discounts are available on quantity purchases by corporations, associations, and others. For details, contact the publisher at the address above.

Orders by U.S. trade bookstores and wholesalers. Please contact Jacobs & Whitehall: Tel: (888) 991-2766 or visit www.jacobsandwhitehall.com.

Printed in the United States of America

Published in 2022

PREFACE

You just bought a brand "new" vehicle. You're excited and brag about it to all your family and friends. You paid an expensive "new" car or motorcycle price, because you didn't want to deal with aggravating and time consuming "used" vehicle problems. You wanted *reliability* and *peace of mind.*

So you start driving your brand "new" vehicle and *suddenly you're surprised that something goes wrong*. The brakes are squealing, the vehicle is hesitating, or even *worse*...it breaks down and you're stuck with your brand "new" car or motorcycle on the side of the road. Despite the inconvenience you do what you're supposed to do and take your "new" vehicle in to be repaired under its warranty. You're thinking to yourself, my vehicle isn't defect free like I thought it would be when I bought it and this situation is causing havoc on my schedule, but surely it will get repaired and then I can get back to my normal life.

After the repair is attempted on your vehicle you get it back, you're driving it, then something *else* goes wrong, or even *worse*, it's the same problem over and over *again*. You feel stuck and think to yourself because the vehicle's being repaired under warranty and they're repairing it for "free" what can I really do?

Well, guess what? The Law is there to *Help YOU*. The Arizona Lemon Law (and other breach of warranty laws) are there to tell the manufacturer *enough is enough* when a vehicle is not produced properly *and* is not repaired properly in a reasonable number of attempts or time.

In fact, the Arizona Legislature decided to add an attorneys' fee provision to the Arizona Lemon Law to help consumers by forcing companies to pay attorneys' fees for successfully resolved Arizona Lemon Law claims so consumers like you could get the help of an attorney. The Legislature made this addition to the Lemon Law because the companies were *not* doing the right thing:

- They were *not* replacing defective vehicles.
- They were *not* giving consumers their money back.
- They were *not* even compensating people fairly!

So if you feel that you've been unfairly *saddled* with a "Lemon" vehicle and are the kind of person who stands up for yourself about it and doesn't take it lying down; if you're tired of being forced to deal with the stress and uncertainty of continuous faulty vehicle problems; if the frustration and inconvenience of numerous or untimely failed repairs is driving you crazy! If you've finally had *ENOUGH*... It's time to Banish your "Lemon" vehicle with the Refund, New Vehicle, or Cash Compensation you Deserve!

Even if you're fired up now and ready to start the process of getting rid of your "Lemon" vehicle, choosing how to pursue a Lemon Law claim isn't easy. Why? Because you're bombarded with misleading advertising and confusing poor information. How do you find a competent, professional Lemon Law attorney (out of all the lawyers and firms marketing their services), and follow the right process to get the maximum compensation you're entitled to and deserve?

You start by reading *this* book. My book will educate you about Lemon Law and Breach of Warranty claims to get you started on a path to being "Lemon" Free. I wrote it to help you better understand these types of consumer protection claims and the recovery process. Now with this information you can make informed, intelligent decisions.

If you have any questions about Lemon Law claims and our Quick, Easy, and FREE 3 Step Out of Court Resolution Process to help consumers like you to get rid of their Lemon vehicles, you're invited to call our Lemon Law Advocates team at (480) 237-2744. We've dedicated our Firm to educating consumers and to *always* putting our clients first with our Fair Fee Guarantee and policy of returning all calls within one business day or less. If your vehicle qualifies under the law, we'll be happy to help you in any way we can.

DEDICATION

This book is dedicated to my grandfather Solomon Bloch. He was a successful doctor who put five kids through college. Sol taught me that it's not the smartest or most talented that win and succeed in life. Potential means nothing without effort and those who are willing to sacrifice and work the hardest are the ones who accomplish the most in life.

My grandfather also taught me to never give up and always keep going despite obstacles or setbacks. Sol practiced what he preached by running multiple marathons in his 50s despite having his legs crushed and almost being killed after being run over by a big rig truck. He will always be a huge inspiration for me.

This book is also dedicated to my amazing team of attorneys and support staff. It wouldn't be possible to provide as much quality service as we do to our clients or to be the highest rated Lemon Law Firm in the country without them.

Disclaimer

This publication is intended to be used for educational purposes only. No legal advice is being given, and no attorney-client relationship is intended to be created by reading this material. The author assumes no liability for any errors or omissions or for how this book or its contents are used or interpreted, or for any consequences resulting directly or indirectly from the use of this book. For legal or any other advice, please consult an experienced attorney or the appropriate expert, who is aware of the specific facts of your case and is knowledgeable in the law in your jurisdiction.

Amar Law Group, PLLC

7001 N. Scottsdale Road
Suite 2060
Scottsdale, AZ, 85253
www.arizonalemonlawamar.com
(480) 887-9924

Testimonials

"Shalev, I want to take a moment to thank you for your professionalism and expediency in helping me get a settlement on my claim. As you know, purchasing a new automobile is an exciting time only to be diminished when it goes back to the dealership time and time again because it has defects. After finding you online and presenting my information, you and your associates immediately took action and began working to help me. Having never filed a claim against a car manufacturer and given the fact that I don't live in your state, I was very hesitant to sign an agreement to proceed forward. Now in hindsight, I am so happy that I did. I found your agreement obligation-free unless there was a settlement, easy to understand and your fees upon settlement were honest and reasonable and, in fact, I have already recommended you to a co-worker! Thank you again."

– Gabrielle Burton

****

"I was represented by Shalev Amar, out of the Tempe, Az. office... Mr. Amar worked diligently on my behalf against an aggressive motor home manufacturer. But finally we prevailed with a decent settlement and an additional warranty on the affected RV parts. I was kept informed as the case proceeded and approved of the final settlement. I would not hesitate to recommend this Attorney Group to family and friends...Thank you and all your staff for handling this matter in a professional manner."

– Adrian Peet

****

"Shalev, I would like to personally thank you and your firm for the help on my 2014 [vehicle]...we are very pleased with the settlement. You were able to work with us and (the manufacturer) and get the best settlement possible for our situation. You were also able to successfully minimize the time needed on our end. We would have no problem recommending you in the future if the time came. Thanks again for all of the help."

– Brian Ritchlin

****

"Shalev, from our first call to your office seeking assistance with our ongoing recreational vehicle issues, we have been treated very professionally by yourself and your associates. You patiently explained our options at the start and throughout the process. Your aggressive pursuit of a fair settlement was instrumental in reaching a satisfactory resolution. Additionally, your personal contact and assistance allowed us to make knowledgeable decisions along the way and in our opinion reach a fair resolution with adequate compensation from the manufacturer. We can say unequivocally that your help was responsible for the successful result and we would recommend your firm's services to anyone experiencing unsatisfactory service or repairs by a recreational vehicle dealership or manufacturer. Thank you."

– Marty Collins

****

"It was a pleasure working with Mr. Shalev Amar. He was very helpful throughout the whole process, he returned my calls in a timely manner, and he answered all of my questions. The staff that answers the phone was always very polite and respectful. I received my check on 2/20/16. I would highly recommend this firm to friends and family and in the event that I need help again I know who to call. Thanks again."

– Yeni Mota

****

TABLE OF CONTENTS

Scottsdale, Arizona Lemon Law Attorney Shalev Amar

When I first went into law, I wanted to be a prosecutor. It took me only a couple of internships to realize prosecution wasn't for me, so I transitioned to civil law.

The first job I got was with a national Lemon Law firm that had a branch in Arizona. When working at this firm, I really liked that we could help people out of their defective vehicle situation. I could look at myself in the mirror, knowing I was helping people who were saddled with a "Lemon" through no fault of their own, and I wasn't hurting anybody.

There were also some things that I really did not like at that firm. The firm seemed to put themselves first, instead of the clients or team members. If the firm got paid its full fee, leadership didn't care what the clients got.

That never sat right with me. It was as though they looked at clients as just a nuisance to get themselves paid and at employees as mere cogs in their money machine.

I believe in always putting your clients first and treating your employees well. Staying true to these beliefs, my original law partner and I left that national firm to go out independently and start a competing Lemon Law Firm.

We opened our own Arizona Lemon Law firm and immediately did things very differently. We decided to always put our clients first.

Eventually, I started my own firm but kept the same practice of always putting clients first.

One example of this is if a maximum out-of-court settlement offer comes in lower than our clients want, but they don't want to escalate to court, we voluntarily agree to cut our Firm's fees per our Fair Fee Guarantee, so the client is able to get additional compensation.

In my view, if you put people first by reducing your fees in a particular case to help your client out, it will come back to you ten-fold in positive reviews and referrals.

I believe in an abundant, infinite universe; there's no reason to have a scarcity mindset, trying to take everything you can out of each Lemon Law claim only for yourself. If you take care of others, they'll take care of you in return.

Arizona Lemon Law Rights: What Consumers Need to Know

Many consumers buying brand-new vehicles don't realize they have substantial rights that are protected by Lemon Laws like the Arizona Lemon Law and the federal Magnuson-Moss Warranty Act.

Often, someone will buy a new vehicle that turns out to be a "Lemon"—a vehicle requiring repeated warranty repairs for substantial defects or conditions, defect repairs that take way too long, or both. Typically, the "Lemon" vehicle has been in the repair shop too many times or for too long because of substantial defects or conditions, like brakes, engine, transmission, suspension, steering, hesitation, vibration, non-starting, dying, etc.

With mass manufacturing, at least a small percentage of vehicles will inevitably come out defective. It fluctuates by manufacturer and year to year, but I would estimate that anywhere from five to ten percent of new vehicles sold could end up qualifying as a "Lemon" every year. In those situations, the manufacturer should accept responsibility for the faulty product instead of letting the consumer who got the short end of the stick stay saddled with the "Lemon" vehicle.

People often don't know the Arizona Lemon Law can help them. Even if they do know, they have no idea what it entails. They are unaware of the Lemon

Law's standards or requirements, and what type of compensation it can get them.

In Arizona, the Lemon Law forces companies to take responsibility for defective vehicles that can't be repaired under warranty within a reasonable number of repair attempts or time and to pay attorney fees for successfully resolved cases.

Unfortunately, many people aren't aware they can basically get a lawyer for free to help them with their defective vehicle out-of-court. So instead of having the situation resolved with a Lemon Law refund, new vehicle replacement, or cash compensation, consumers unwittingly trade out of their vehicle for a substantial loss because they're fed up with dealing with defects and repeated or untimely repairs. Although getting rid of the problem vehicle as quickly as possible is understandable under the circumstances, it is an unwise choice given the potential compensation that is missed out on and also lets the manufacturer of the "Lemon" vehicle off the hook scot-free.

Adding insult to injury, "Lemon" vehicle consumers often are forced to roll over a very high negative loan balance into a new vehicle purchase. This can easily happen because even without any defect problems, just by driving a vehicle off the lot it can decrease in value by 10%.

People buy new vehicles because they don't want to deal with used vehicle problems and pay a premium price for a new vehicle because they want reliability. They need to know they can get from point A to point B, whether it's to work, school, family functions, social activities, or wherever they need to be in their new vehicle, without breakdowns or defect issues. That's why it is very unfair to buy a brand "new" vehicle in good faith and end up with the equivalent of a run-down "used" vehicle worth substantially less.

The few Lemon vehicle purchasers who try to hold the manufacturer responsible for a defective vehicle on their own may reach out to the company with the intention of obtaining an adequate resolution, but most of the time they receive very minimal compensation or nothing at all.

Even compensation for a month or two of payments, a 3-month warranty extension, or free oil changes that a manufacturer representative may sometimes provide a Lemon vehicle consumer is not anything close to what the Arizona Lemon Law warrants.

In Arizona, you are entitled to an Arizona Lemon Law buyback or a new vehicle replacement, sticker price to sticker price. Arizona also provides alternative warranty laws, allowing compensation for diminution in value—the payment for the difference in worth between the new vehicle that was purchased versus the defective run-down vehicle actually received. After all, you didn't get what you paid for, and the new versus old price difference could be thousands of dollars, not just a month or two of payments.

In the rare cases where the company agrees to reacquire the vehicle from a consumer without an attorney involved, often it doesn't follow all the requirements of the Arizona Lemon Law. The company may charge you massive amounts of money for the use of the vehicle, much higher than the law would call for. The company may not compensate you for certain charges, like financing and other expenses put towards the vehicle, that should be reimbursed under the Lemon Law.

So as you can see, even in the small percentage of cases where companies do the right thing by reacquiring a "Lemon" vehicle, they're still usually not fully complying with the law. They give with one hand and take away with the other!

When it comes to being compensated for buying a defective vehicle, it is essential to know your rights and the standards of the Arizona Lemon Law as well as other breach of warranty laws. This book will reveal your rights and highlight the essential details of the Arizona Lemon Law and other applicable warranty laws.

CHAPTER 1

THE HISTORY OF THE LEMON LAW

State Lemon Laws generally started being passed in the 1980s due to a wide range of State laws and court decisions regarding what consumers could be compensated for or not with defective "Lemon" vehicles.

Before State Lemon Laws were enacted, the legal standard for getting compensated for a defective "Lemon" vehicle was based on State versions of the Uniformed Commercial Code (UCC) and breach of warranty common law (judicial precedent).

UCC claims are very complicated, having many different complex elements. With so many legal elements needed to be proven to prevail on a UCC based claim, even if even one element was not established that would lead to losing the entire case. That made it burdensome for consumers to get rid of or be compensated for their defective "Lemon" vehicles.

Before State Lemon Laws were passed, consumers would buy warrantied vehicles and the warranties weren't worth the paper they were written on. Defective vehicle warranties were difficult to enforce under a patchwork of contradictory, conflicting, and confusing State laws (see above) even when "Lemon" vehicles couldn't be repaired in a reasonable number of attempts or reasonable time. Because of this complicated legal minefield, consumers were frequently (and unfairly) trapped in "Lemon" vehicles or forced to trade out of them for a loss.

In the late 70s the tide began to turn in favor of consumers when a statute called the Magnuson-Moss Warranty Act ("MMWA") was passed at the federal level. Most State Lemon Laws are now roughly modeled on the federal Magnuson-Moss Warranty Act's section regarding full warranties (15 U.S.C. § 2304), but they tend to have more teeth to protect consumers of defective vehicles than the MMWA.

The MMWA makes a distinction between full warranties and limited warranties. The MMWA requirement for full warranties is what State Lemon Laws are modeled after because it expressly pertains to a reasonable number of repair attempts being required to complete repairs otherwise there is legal violation entitling the consumer to compensation.

The challenge with the MMWA is that most vehicle warranties are limited warranties. The statute is not explicit about what the standard is for breach of limited warranties, as opposed to full warranties. This lack of clarity led to another patchwork of legal standards between the States, where courts would look at State warranty and UCC laws to determine what is a breach of a limited warranty under the federal act.

Fortunately, State Lemon Laws provide clearer black-and-white standards of Lemon Law violations for unreasonably lengthy or numerous limited warranty vehicle repairs and how you can be compensated due to those violations.

Currently, all 50 states have some type of Lemon Law to assist consumers of defective warranted vehicles, including in Arizona.

Originally the Arizona Lemon Law was passed without an attorneys' fee provision. As a result, companies took advantage of people and did not do everything they were legally required to in Lemon vehicle situations.

In response, Arizona, which is not always the most consumer-friendly State, decided to add an attorney's fee provision, so consumers could hire an attorney to protect their legal rights and make sure they get fair Lemon Law enforcement and results.

Under A.R.S. 44-1265(B) consumers can get their reasonable attorneys' fees paid for by the other side if they prevail in a Lemon Law action. Under Arizona case law, a settlement is considered to be prevailing in a Lemon Law claim.

How Is a "Lemon" Vehicle Defined?

According to the Arizona Lemon Law, for a vehicle to qualify as a "Lemon," first, there needs to be a substantial defect, non-conformity, or condition; it can't just be something trivial.

For example, if you have a rattle in a cup-holder, that's not going to qualify because it is not substantial and has no major effect on the proper operation of your vehicle.

The Arizona Lemon Law requires substantial impairment in use and value to the consumer and it's nearly impossible to argue objectively or subjectively that a cup-holder qualifies as substantial impairment.

On the other hand, there are some defects, non-conformities, or conditions that are obviously substantial to any consumer:

- Brakes
- Transmission
- Steering
- Engine
- Suspension
- Stalling out/Dying in transit
- Non-Starting
- Hesitation upon acceleration
- Vibration

If your vehicle's brakes don't work and you can't stop your vehicle, that's substantial, perhaps even life-threatening.

If your vehicle doesn't start, that's substantial impairment in use and value because you could be stuck in the middle of nowhere.

If your vehicle cuts out or hesitates while driving, that's a substantial safety issue that clearly impairs use and value.

There are defects, non-conformities, or conditions that occur in vehicles which are more in a gray area that may or may not be considered substantial impairment in use and value to the consumer. Some examples are a defective stereo system, cracked windshield, or window leaks.

Whether these defects qualify as substantial impairment in use and value is very fact-specific, and it depends on the severity and actual impairing results of those defects.

Moreover, the more a vehicle defect or condition happens and the more times it gets repeatedly repaired, the more likely the problem could qualify as substantial impairment in use and value of the vehicle.

In other words, when gray area defects occur over and over again the contention that they are substantial is strengthened, based on them repeatedly happening and continually inconveniencing a consumer. This obviously has the effect of impairing the vehicle's use and devaluing it to the consumer.

While there is no specific standard to how many repair attempts or how much time in the repair shop qualifies your vehicle as a "Lemon," there are guideposts called presumptions.

The Arizona Lemon Law sets two presumptions for determining if a repair history is unreasonable (one of the main factors for determining if a vehicle is legally a "Lemon" along with substantial impairment) within the first two years or 24,000 miles ownership:

1. Four or more repairs for the same defect or condition and the defect continues to exist.
2. 30 or more cumulative days in the repair shop for the same or different issues, including separate repair attempts collectively equaling 30 days.

The presumptions are not required to be reached to have a valid Arizona Lemon Law claim, but if they are met, the presumptions shift the burden of proof from the consumer to the manufacturer. That means a tie about whether the repair history is legally unreasonable goes to the consumer.

Usually, the consumer who brings the claim must prove the elements of the claim by a preponderance of the evidence. This means the consumer doesn't have to prove the case beyond a reasonable doubt—it's not a criminal case—their argument just has to be one point stronger than the manufacturer's defense to win. It's like a basketball game where both sides score points, but the one that scores the most points wins.

By shifting the burden of proof to the other side, it's up to the manufacturer to have more points than the consumer. The manufacturer has the burden to prove the repair history is not unreasonable.

However, the vehicle repairs are listed in the repair records of the repairing dealer, who is the authorized warranty repair agent for the manufacturer. It is difficult for the manufacturer to argue against its repair agent's repair records to claim the repairs are somehow reasonable.

It's important to reiterate that you can have fewer repairs or days out of service than indicated in the presumptions succeed in an Arizona Lemon Law claim. If the number of warranty repairs or time to complete repairs are unreasonable under the circumstances, the vehicle can still qualify as a "Lemon."

Typically, in our view, if there are at least three repeat repairs or 25-plus days in the repair shop for a substantial defect, non-conformity, or condition within two years or 24,000 miles, that should qualify as a "Lemon" vehicle.

There is even a rational argument that when a vehicle has very low mileage that even fewer repairs or days in the repair shop could qualify. Perhaps the vehicle only has 5,000 miles, and the brakes do not work, causing near-crashes. In that situation it is possible that even two repairs could qualify this vehicle as a "Lemon" because the defect and its unsafe consequences in such low mileage are so substantial and recurrent.

Although it's very fact-specific when it comes to this gray area, it's only logical that the more substantial and dangerous the vehicle defect or condition is, the less repairs are needed to prove the repair history is unreasonable under the Lemon Law. Again, it really depends on if the repair history is unreasonable under the circumstances.

CHAPTER 2

WHEN IS A VEHICLE CONSIDERED TO BE A "LEMON"?

How long it takes to consider a vehicle to be a "Lemon" differs from owner to owner. Some vehicles have tons of problems from the start, and the consumer gets fed up pretty quickly after making the vehicle purchase.

Other vehicles are like a slow drip, with a defect problem every few months. In that situation it could take longer for consumers to feel saddled with a "Lemon" vehicle.

In either scenario, when enough is enough, the consumer gets upset about making payments on a brand-new vehicle that can't be used trouble free as intended because of its defects and can't be used at all when it is repeatedly in the repair shop.

There's no exact number of warranty repair attempts or time out of service for repairs required to be covered under the Arizona Lemon Law. Ultimately, your vehicle's repair history to address substantial defects and conditions must be unreasonable under the circumstances to qualify.

There is an Arizona Lemon Law burden shifting presumption of 4 or more repair attempts for the same defect or condition within the earlier of two years or 24,000 miles of ownership, but that is just a legal standard that helps a consumer prove a claim. It is not a set in stone requirement to qualify for Lemon Law coverage.

In our view, after having dealt with 1000s of Lemon Law claims, at least three repair attempts under warranty to repair a substantial defect, non-conformity, or condition is likely to be legally unreasonable.

One caveat to this is something that could cause death or serious bodily injury. A sensible argument could be made that two repair attempts under warranty are unreasonable if you would be risking your life driving a "Lemon" vehicle with a defect issue that has not been adequately repaired.

Similarly, although there is no particular days out of service by reason of warranty repair time requirement to have a valid Arizona Lemon Law claim, the vehicle must have spent an unreasonable time in the repair shop.

There is an Arizona Lemon Law burden of proof shifting presumption of 30 days out of service by reason of warranty repair within the earlier of two years or 24,000 miles of ownership, but again that is a legal standard that is designed to help a consumer prove a claim. It is not an actual requirement for a vehicle to qualify as a "Lemon."

We believe that 25 or more days in the repair shop in under two years or 24,000 miles of ownership is also unreasonable. That's well over three and a half weeks repairing dealer without your vehicle and you shouldn't have to go that long without your vehicle.

Do the Arizona Lemon Law and the Federal Lemon Law Cover All Vehicles?

Some limitations exclude certain vehicles from being covered by the Arizona Lemon Law.

For one, the vehicle cannot be more than 10,000 pounds. Vehicles over this weight limit could be protected under other warranty laws, but not the Arizona Lemon Law.

The other issue that may disqualify a vehicle from being covered by the Arizona Lemon Law is the defect or nonconformity repairs must be done within the first two years or 24,000 miles of ownership. If the warranty repairs start after the earlier of two years or 24,000 miles of ownership, those would not be subject to Arizona Lemon Law coverage.

The one exception to this time and mileage limit is with respect to the presumption of having four more repair attempts for the same defect or condition, and the defect continues to exist. If there are additional related repairs after the two-year or 24,000-mile period, those repairs can be used to demonstrate the continued existence of the previously unsuccessfully repaired defect.

If the vehicle repairs are under warranty but occur after the two-year or 24,000-mile period, other warranty laws, like the federal Magnuson-Moss Warranty Act may apply.

The main difference between federal and Arizona Lemon Laws is what type of compensation the consumer can get.

The consumer can receive a vehicle repurchase or replacement plus attorney's fees under the Arizona Lemon Law.

Under the Magnuson-Moss Warranty Act, consumers can get diminution in value cash compensation—a partial refund for having overpaid for a vehicle. This cash compensation is provided with the consumer keeping the product. The federal law also entitles the consumer to seek attorneys' fees for this type of claim.

Vehicles that are purchased used in a private sale might possibly be disqualified from Arizona Lemon Law coverage, but this is more of a gray area. If the "Lemon" vehicle is covered under manufacturer's warranty and the repairs are done in the first two years or 24,000 miles of ownership, it could be argued that it is subject to Arizona Lemon Law coverage since the statute does not specifically exclude private party sales and is also a remedial statute that should be broadly interpreted to protect consumers.

The controlling issue is whether the defective vehicle is covered under the manufacturer's warranty and fits the time limits of either an Arizona Lemon Law or Magnuson-Moss Warranty Act claim. Most private sales will not meet these requirements because they tend to be for used vehicles that are old enough to be outside the manufacturer's warranty coverage period.

Finally, the Arizona Lemon Law requires that vehicles be designed primarily for transportation on public highways.

The Magnuson-Moss Warranty Act on the other hand, only requires that the vehicle be a consumer product, so it covers a wider array of vehicles than the Arizona Lemon Law.

The additional types of vehicle covered by the Magnuson-Moss Warranty Act include 5th Wheels, Travel Trailers, Offroad Vehicles, and Boats.

CHAPTER 3

ARIZONA LEMON LAW COVERAGE FOR USED VEHICLES

Arizona Lemon Law coverage for used vehicles isn't great. Here's why…

For basic Arizona Lemon Law coverage pertaining to manufacturer's vehicle warranties (with the ability to seek a repurchase or new replacement vehicle), your vehicle's defect or nonconformity repairs must be done under warranty within the first two years or 24,000 miles of ownership.

If your vehicle warranty repairs start after two years or 24,000 miles of ownership, those would not be subject to Arizona Lemon Law coverage although they may be covered under the federal Magnuson-Moss Warranty Act, which pertains to the entire duration of the vehicle's warranty.

Technically speaking, a used vehicle that has less than 2 years or 24,000 miles of use when it is purchased would still be covered under the Arizona Lemon Law so long as the warranty repair history (too many repairs or too much time out of service for repair) for a substantial defect or condition occurs before the expiration of that time period.

Unfortunately, consumers who purchase a used vehicle with an expired manufacturer's warranty, have very limited Arizona Lemon Law coverage under A.R.S. § 44-1267. Here's what that entails:

There is a 15-day, 500-mile implied warranty of merchantability for all used cars in Arizona under A.R.S. § 44-1267. The implied warranty requires any repairs that have to be done within the first 15 days or

500 miles of ownership, be done at no more than a $25 charge to the consumer, otherwise the consumer may have a viable claim. A.R.S. § 44-1267 also has some labeling requirements on vehicles to notify consumers of the 15day/500 mile implied warranty.

If a vehicle is reacquired as a "Lemon," meaning it is bought back or replaced by the manufacturer under the Lemon Law, there are additional Arizona Lemon Law coverages under A.R.S. § 44-1266 if the vehicle is resold to a consumer. These reacquired Lemon vehicles are generally sold by manufacturers at auction where dealers will buy the vehicles and then resell them to consumers.

Dealerships are allowed to sell reacquired Lemon vehicles under the law, but if they do, the dealers must provide written notification affixed to the vehicle and have the consumer sign a disclosure acknowledging the vehicle was previously reacquired by the manufacturer as a "Lemon." If those requirements are violated, then the consumer has an Arizona Lemon Law claim that could be brought against the dealership.

If the vehicle's manufacturer did not affix the reacquired Lemon notification to the vehicle in the first place, then a claim could be made against the manufacturer under A.R.S. § 44-1266.

Often times a consumer doesn't discover that a previously reacquired Lemon vehicle was purchased until the vehicle is sold or traded out of. Due to that, we highly recommend that you demand to see the entire Carfax on any used vehicle prior to agreeing to purchase it.

That way, you can decline to make the purchase based on the vehicle being a reacquired Lemon. If you still decide to buy the vehicle, you can at least request that the price be lowered to account for the vehicle being labeled a Lemon.

Are There Downsides to My Vehicle Qualifying as a Lemon?

As long as the manufacturer reacquires your vehicle under the Arizona Lemon Law there are no downsides to having it determined to be a "Lemon."

By reacquiring the defective vehicle, the manufacturer either provides you a Lemon Law Buyback, or replaces your vehicle with a brand-new vehicle that has a similar sticker price with you keeping the same loan terms if there is a loan balance remaining.

Moreover, when the manufacturer reacquires your "Lemon" vehicle, it becomes the company's responsibility to deal with it including properly attaching written notification to the vehicle of its reacquired "Lemon" status.

On the other hand, if you have a Lemon vehicle and the manufacturer does not reacquire it (or at least provide cash compensation for the vehicle's unreasonable repair history), the downside for you is the value of your vehicle will likely decrease.

In this day and age, it's fairly easy to pull up a vehicle warranty repair history on Carfax. If you try to trade your vehicle in, a dealer can ding the vehicle's trade-in value. Even in a private party sale, a potential buyer who sees the vehicle's repair history probably won't give you maximum value for it because the vehicle is potentially unreliable.

Because of that, it is a big financial mistake not to seek compensation for your "Lemon" vehicle.

CHAPTER 4

MY VEHICLE IS A "LEMON." WHERE DO I START?

Once you suspect you have a "Lemon" vehicle, the first step is to ensure you have all of the vehicle repair records/repair orders from repairing dealers, leaving nothing out that was done to diagnose and repair your vehicle as well as accurately documenting the time your vehicle was in the repair shop. These repair records are the number one piece of evidence in Arizona Lemon Law cases.

Anybody can claim they have a "Lemon," but you need written documentation backing up your defect and repair complaints about your vehicle. Dealership repair orders are great evidence of that because they are business records produced at the time repairs are undertaken by the actual warranty repair agents of the vehicle's manufacturer.

If any repair records are missing, they should be requested from the repairing dealer(s). When doing this, it's very important not to mention the Arizona Lemon Law or Arizona Lemon Law Attorneys.

Here's why:

Although the Arizona Lemon Law, which pertains to unreasonably numerous or lengthy warranty defect repairs, applies to your vehicle's manufacturer, the dealer has an ongoing business relationship with the manufacturer. Because of that, dealers will often try to protect the producer of a Lemon vehicle.

After all, the repairing dealer sells the manufacturer's vehicles and gets paid by the manufacturer to do warranty repairs. So if the dealer believes there is a potential Arizona Lemon Law claim brewing, it will do what it can to look out for and protect the manufacturer.

As the consumer, you're under no duty to volunteer that you're considering an Arizona Lemon Law or breach of warranty claim if you're requesting missing vehicle repair records—that is none of the dealership's business. Often, just asking for a copy of the repair records is sufficient; the dealer won't ask you anything further.

If the dealer does ask "why?", you can easily reply, "I just want to have complete records on file of what's been done to my vehicle." That is all you really need to say.

If the dealer pushes beyond that answer, you can add, "I'm having repeat problems, and I don't want to be blamed for not seeking repairs if the problem reoccurs or potentially be accused of misusing my vehicle."

Remember, you're not required to tell the dealer your life story and you have a right to obtain the repair records for your vehicle as the owner of it.

After getting the repair records, we recommend visiting our website to get educated about the out-of-court Lemon Law resolution process.

You can also get educated on details of the Arizona Lemon Law and the Federal Lemon Law to see if your vehicle may qualify.

If you believe there's even a chance you qualify, you should call our firm toll-free at (866) 904-2627 or locally at (480) 237-2744.

We offer a Free No-obligation Lemon Law Evaluation. During this consultation, we'll collect information about your vehicle.

If it appears the vehicle may qualify under the Arizona Lemon Law, or other breach of warranty laws, we'll ask to review your repair records. The records can be emailed, faxed, or even texted to us, as long as legible pictures of the records are taken with a smartphone.

We'll evaluate the repair records, and if your vehicle qualifies, we set up a time to discuss your rights and compensation options.

Should I Continue to Make Payments on my Lemon Vehicle?

If you are required to make payments on your vehicle because you signed a financing agreement for it, you should continue making them, even if your vehicle is determined to be a "Lemon." Here's why…

Under the law, two wrongs don't make a right. You have a contractual obligation to make payments on the vehicle until a Lemon Law resolution is (hopefully) obtained.

The good news is that you're not just stuck making payments on a "Lemon" until it's paid off if you take the right action by seeking Free Out-of-Court Lemon Law help. After all, there is a process under the Lemon Law for you to get your vehicle bought back or replaced.

Specifically, the Arizona Lemon Law gives you the ability to get a Lemon Law Buyback, which will provide a refund for your purchase, minus mileage, and typically a payoff of any outstanding loan balance. You can also potentially get a new vehicle replacement valued sticker price to sticker price, keeping the same loan, or cash compensation for breach of warranty in the alternative.

However, the law does not support taking matters into your own hands and violating your financing agreement. That would cause you major problems…

Not paying on your loan could ruin your credit and lead to your vehicle being repossessed. Judicial opinions say you can't seek an Arizona Lemon Law Buyback or new vehicle replacement if you don't have the "Lemon" vehicle to give back to the manufacturer. If the bank owns your vehicle, you won't have it to give back as the Arizona Lemon Law requires. In other words, if the vehicle is repoed for non-payment, you've unintentionally killed your Arizona Lemon Law case.

Don't get us wrong, it's very challenging to pay for something that's not working properly. You feel ripped-off and justifiably so.

Regardless, the proper way to deal with this unfair situation is by pursuing your Arizona Lemon Law and breach of warranty rights, not letting the manufacturer off the hook while ruining your credit. Simply put, stopping payments on your vehicle will backfire severely and is shooting yourself in the foot. That's why we strongly recommended not to stop making monthly payments if you have a "Lemon" vehicle.

Here's what you should do instead…

Invest a small amount of time (typically 30 minutes or less over an average of 3 months) in pursuing a Free Out-of-Court Arizona Lemon Law Resolution Process with Amar Law Group that has a 95% Success Rate.

This will require a bit of patience, but you'll have the opportunity to obtain an Arizona Lemon Law Buyback or New Vehicle Replacement.

Alternatively, you could get substantial cash compensation while keeping your credit intact and holding the manufacturer financially responsible for producing your defective "Lemon" vehicle.

Instead of getting mad and doing something understandable but foolish, get even as you're legally entitled to.

CHAPTER 5

SHOULD I CONTACT THE MANUFACTURER OF MY "LEMON" VEHICLE OR HIRE AN ATTORNEY?

We strongly recommend contacting an Arizona Lemon Law attorney before directly contacting the manufacturer about your "Lemon" vehicle. Here's why…

Having a defective "Lemon" vehicle is not like buying a defective TV where you can take it back to BestBuy, and they just give you another new TV. With defective vehicles, that is not the way it works because they are much more expensive and complicated products than home appliances.

If you decide to contact the manufacturer on your own about your Lemon vehicle, you're going into the Lion's Den. Without substantial prior experience in these types of cases or the law in general, you can't possibly know all the pitfalls to avoid or the standards and procedures to follow.

The manufacturer's customer service departments are often staffed by attorneys or representatives that have been legally trained in this area of law. These representatives are extensively trained (and retrained) to minimize the company's costs and get you to make legal admissions that could hurt your claim and minimize your recovery.

Manufacturers know out of every ten people who contact them with a legitimate Lemon Law claim, maybe only one or two will actually hire an attorney to pursue the Arizona Lemon Law, even if they threaten to hire an attorney. With this knowledge, their goal is to resolve the issue as cheaply as possible.

That's why they'll often try to sweet-talk you and not provide any compensation that is even close to what you're legally entitled to. When offered, the compensation is usually just a month or two of payments, some free maintenance, or a short warranty extension.

This minimal compensation usually comes with a huge catch like signing a release that waives all of your rights to compensation and erasing all of the past repair issues you've experienced with your vehicle.

Even if the manufacturer representatives do offer you something the Arizona Lemon Law says you are eligible for, frequently, they don't offer you everything you're legally entitled to—the devil is in the details.

There is a famous saying, "The person who represents himself has a fool for a client." That's why even when attorneys have a legal issue to deal with, they will rarely if ever represent themselves.

An attorney's job is to be logical and objective about legal standards and procedures that apply to a particular situation. When you're directly involved in a matter, it's extremely difficult to be logical and objective rather than riled up and personally offended. You're more likely to be emotional and upset about the situation—which is justified—but could lead to making very grave legal mistakes.

In view of the above, it makes sense to talk to an Arizona Lemon Law attorney first when you have a Lemon vehicle. In our firm, we provide Free No-Obligation Lemon Law Evaluations so it costs you nothing to have an attorney evaluate your case.

For our cases that qualify for Free Lemon Law Help, 95% resolve out-of-court with our Quick, Easy, and Free, 3-Step Lemonaid Process. So it doesn't cost you anything out-of-pocket to have our attorneys argue and advocate on your behalf out-of-court.

The attorney's job, as your fiduciary, is to act in your best financial interest and to work hard for the best possible outcome.

On the other hand, the manufacturer has zero fiduciary duty to you and will do what is in its best financial interest, not yours.

So don't make the mistake of contacting a vehicle manufacturer on your own before consulting with an experienced Lemon Law attorney about your defective vehicle situation.

Chapter 6

Is it Too Late to File a Lemon Law Claim?

The statute of limitations to file a Lemon Law claim varies by State. In Arizona, you have six months from the time you hit 24,000 miles on the odometer or after two years of ownership, whichever comes first, to file an action in court under the Arizona Lemon Law.

Even if your vehicle appears to qualify for Arizona Lemon Law help you might think you should wait to see if problems keep occurring with your

"Lemon" vehicle. Some people prefer not to rock the boat unless they absolutely have to. Keep in mind though that you didn't do anything wrong here when you bought your new vehicle in good faith expecting it would operate reliably like a new vehicle should.

The Arizona Lemon Law is not punitive towards Lemon vehicle manufacturers. You're not seeking millions of dollars from these companies when pursuing an Arizona Lemon Law claim. You just want the manufacturer to accept responsibility by taking the Lemon vehicle back or compensating you fairly. However, if you wait, your Lemon Law claim could either be timed out or significantly hurt.

At the end of the day, there's really no good reason to wait. It's not a good idea to sit back and wait to see if the repair was finally successful this time. The past is the best predictor of the future. If you've had frequent or repeated problems with your vehicle in the past, what makes you think it's finally going to be repaired? It's highly unlikely the past warranty repairs will prevent more defect and repair issues from occurring in the future.

Just waiting a couple of months can be the difference between having a valid Arizona Lemon Law claim or not. Once that time is up, it's up, no matter how many repairs you've had to deal with or how long your vehicle was unusable while in the repair shop.

Moreover, waiting gives the manufacturer an argument it would not otherwise have against you. The argument is that since a couple of months have passed, the vehicle is properly repaired, and you shouldn't be compensated as much if you make a claim. Maybe you shouldn't be compensated at all because all's well that ends well. Those arguments are nonsense because all of the hassle and inconvenience you've been through, not to mention wasted time dealing with repairs that you'll never get back. Regardless, these are the types of arguments the companies still make.

With the federal Magnuson-Moss Warranty Act, you have more time. The federal law is based on the duration of your vehicle's warranty. It's still not something you want to wait on. Time is your enemy here. As each week goes on without problems, your case gets weaker and could cost you the compensation you're entitled to. Again you may potentially receive substantially less compensation than you would have if you didn't wait.

Can The Manufacturer Refuse A Refund Or Replacement Of A Lemon Car?

In the out-of-court negotiation process, the manufacturer can technically refuse to take back a "Lemon" vehicle even if it is clear that it's repair history exceeds the 4 or more repair attempts for the same defect or 30 days out of service Lemon Law presumptions, but that doesn't happen too often. We take measures to ensure this doesn't occur for egregious Lemon Law matters we handle:

1. We only take on legitimate claims. As part of our Free Lemon Law evaluation, we assess whether you have a valid claim and that the vehicle qualifies for Arizona Lemon Law help. We're not going to waste your time or our time on non-qualifying matters. If your vehicle does not

qualify (and does not appear as it would qualify in the future), we will not take on the matter.

2. Going to trial costs the manufacturer a ton of money. Often the company agrees to settle because it would be very difficult to defend a valid Lemon Law claim in court. The manufacturers know, if our clients are on board, we're one of the firms that will sue if they unfairly deny a claim. We've defeated them in trial before. Trials in these cases cost a massive amount in attorney's fees that they have to pay if they lose. They have to pay a defense attorney a ton of money, pay our attorney's fees, plus buy back or replace your vehicle under the Arizona Lemon Law if they lose. Even if a manufacturer wins, it pays the defense attorney money that often is two, three, even four or more times the cost of your vehicle. It is a poor financial decision.

These companies have a high financial incentive to amicably resolve legitimate claims out-of-court without a lawsuit. Still, they do have the right to refuse to repurchase or replace the vehicle. When they do, they're often not denying the Lemon Law claim outright; they're just refusing to reacquire the vehicle. Generally, when this happens, the company thinks it has a defense to the Lemon Law claim, like a certain time in the repair shop shouldn't count, or some of the repairs are your fault.

If they think the vehicle shouldn't qualify under the Arizona Lemon Law as a "Lemon" for some reason, they'll usually offer cash compensation, which is another way of accepting at least some responsibility for the problems you've had with your vehicle. In some cases, cash compensation is even a better deal for you than a Lemon Law Buyback depending on the trade-in value of the vehicle. Here's why...

In Arizona, a Lemon Law Buyback includes a subtraction for mileage. If you get cash compensation and decide to trade out of your vehicle, depending on the trade-in value of your vehicle and what you owe on the loan, it might come out to a better financial deal for you, especially if your vehicle has higher mileage (e.g., 10,000, 15,000, 20,000 or more miles).

If your vehicle finally ends up properly repaired and you decide to keep it, you have money for your aggravation and for overpaying for the product. You can use that money for whatever you want, to pay down the vehicle, or for another purpose that you deem fit.

CHAPTER 7

AM I GOING TO BE STUCK WITH MY LEMON?

If your vehicle qualifies under the Arizona Lemon Law, the manufacturer has three options to make it right to you out-of-court:

- Buy Back the Lemon vehicle from you
- Replace the Lemon vehicle with a new one that you've chosen
- Compensate you for breach of warranty

When it comes to our 3-Step Out-of-Court Lemonaid Resolution Process, both sides must agree on the best solution. If the manufacturer agrees your vehicle is a Lemon, they typically offer to buy it back from you or replace it with a new vehicle.

The way a Buyback works under the Arizona Lemon Law, is that the company pays you everything you've paid towards the vehicle, including financing charges, tax/title/license, and pays off any outstanding loan balance, minus an offset for mileage.

Unfortunately, that usage offset cannot be zero in Arizona. It is usually calculated at cents per mile that both sides agree to. The Arizona Lemon Law doesn't specify a formula for mileage. It just references a "reasonable" offset.

Reasonable in the context of settlement is what both sides agree on. We obviously argue mileage should be as low as possible, and the other side wants the mileage to be as high as possible. We always negotiate the mileage offset to be as low as possible, and it's up to you whether you approve the mileage deduction or not. Typically, both sides ultimately agree to an amount they can live with.

For example, if a vehicle has 10,000 miles on it and mileage rate offered is 30 cents per mile, $3,000 would be subtracted from your refund if you agree that is a reasonable amount based on the cost of your vehicle.

The way new vehicle replacements work is MSRP value to MSRP value—that is, Sticker Price to Sticker Price. If you have a loan, you keep the same loan payment terms and swap out the Lemon vehicle for comparable new vehicle; this is called a substitution of collateral. If a new vehicle replacement is offered, you will search for an acceptable replacement vehicle (from the same manufacturer brand) to replace your Lemon vehicle.

You basically get a credit for your sticker price, so we recommend searching for a replacement vehicle that matches as closely as possible in price. If the sticker price matches, you don't have to pay anything for your new vehicle. If the sticker price is higher for the new replacement vehicle, you must pay the difference out of pocket. If the sticker price on the replacement vehicle is lower though, they don't refund you the difference, so it doesn't make sense to choose a lower cost replacement.

In Arizona, with Lemon Law Buybacks and vehicle replacements, manufacturers are not required to pay you for aftermarket add-ons—options added to your vehicle that are made by companies who are not the vehicle's original manufacturer, such as a stereo, lift kit, tires, or rims.

You won't be paid for those added-on features by the manufacturer, so you can remove them from the vehicle and transfer them to your new replacement or you can sell them.

Keep in mind the "Lemon" vehicle that's being reacquired should be put back to stock as much as possible. You can't just give them a stripped-down vehicle that doesn't work properly. If you do that you could be charged for the missing original manufacturer's components.

Other items are that are typically not recoverable under the Arizona Lemon Law are extended warranties provided by third-party companies and sold by the dealer, maintenance plans sold by the dealer, and gap insurance. You can get a prorated refund from those particular companies if the service plans are cancelled, but we recommend not seeking that until there is a finalized deal.

An alternative out-of-court resolution to a Lemon Law Buyback or replacement is cash compensation for breach of warranty with you keeping the vehicle. This type of compensation is not written into the Arizona Lemon Law (it is a type of compensation for a similar claim called breach of warranty), but the legal system generally promotes compromise so long both sides agree to it.

This cash compensation is for having overpaid for the vehicle and your inconvenience. It can be an attractive option depending (obviously) on the amount of money offered and on if your vehicle appears to be properly fixed.

There's no specific formula for cash compensation in Lemon Law or breach of warranty matters, but the easiest way to look at it is New versus Used. You paid for a new vehicle, but you got the equivalent of a used, run-down vehicle due to its defects and repair history. You should get reimbursed for the value gap because your vehicle should have cost less when you bought it if its defect and repair issues were foreseeable.

With each out-of-court settlement option (Lemon Law repurchase or replacement; cash compensation), you are entitled to seek attorneys' fees as well as part of the overall settlement.

Although manufacturers generally do not differentiate between attorneys' fees and compensation to you when making cash compensation offers where you keep your vehicle, attorneys' fees are included in such offers. Otherwise, the offers would be substantially lower.

If you no longer want your vehicle, you can trade it in if a cash compensation settlement is reached and the vehicle is kept. Since the settlement is confidential, your vehicle does not actually get tagged or labeled as a "Lemon" even if you may feel that that's what the vehicle is. You can trade-in the vehicle per normal without there being any indication the vehicle is a Lemon on Carfax or any other online database.

With that being said, your vehicle's repair history may affect the trade-in value. However, past consumers have told us that the trade-in value is affected more with an individual private buyer by this than with a dealer.

The reason is, that the dealer looks at the current condition of your vehicle. If the vehicle seems to be in a good state of repair and appears to be fixed, typically, they will not reduce the vehicle's value much based on the repair history although, this varies from dealer to dealer.

The last thing you should do is scrap your Lemon vehicle. There is simply no real need to scrap a vehicle when it turns out to be a "Lemon" because you can seek Lemon Law compensation as described above.

Even if your vehicle is not reacquired by the manufacturer and you settle for cash compensation it is still not advisable to scrap the vehicle. Often a dealership will give you a better value for your vehicle than a scrapyard, even if the vehicle is in a state of disrepair. The dealer that accepts your vehicle as a trade-in will try to recondition the vehicle and then sell it for a higher price.

CHAPTER 8

WHEN SHOULD I CONTACT A LEMON LAW ATTORNEY?

When you realize you've purchased a defective "Lemon" vehicle, it's best to bring in an experienced Arizona Lemon Law attorney right away—the sooner, the better.

When we consult with a potential client to review a potential Lemon Law matter, we need a few pieces of information:

- Year, make, and model of the vehicle.

- Current mileage of the vehicle.
- Defect repair issues.
- Number of times each defect or condition in the vehicle has been repaired.
- How much total time the vehicle has spent in the repair shop.

The main thing the consumer needs to do is gather complete records of the vehicle's defect repair history to complete the Free Lemon Law Evaluation. This information is the main determinant in whether a vehicle qualifies as a potential "Lemon."

Call Amar Law Group

At Amar Law Group, we are different from most other Lemon Law firms. We pride ourselves in putting our clients first and being accessible by keeping open lines of communication.

Our Fair Fee Guarantee is also designed to put our client's needs first. If we receive a low max cash compensation offer and the client doesn't want to go to court, often our flat fee ends up being more than the client gets. If that occurs, we automatically cut our fee giving our client at least an equal amount of compensation from the settlement. We're unaware of any other Lemon Law Firm that has this kind of guarantee. There are even limited circumstances where we're under no obligation to cut our fee, and we still do so to help our clients out.

We believe if we take care of our clients, they'll refer us new clients who are friends, family or acquaintances, and leave us positive reviews.

We know how stressful it is to be stuck with a "Lemon" vehicle. It creates uncertainly, anxiety, and feelings of what's going to go wrong next or that shouldn't be happening with a brand-new product.

We do our utmost to help people out of this situation through an Arizona Lemon Law buyback or new vehicle replacement, or at least a cash compensation.

We also seek for our attorney's fees to be paid by the manufacturer as part of a settlement agreement in out-of-court matters. If it is a cash compensation settlement, then our fees come out of the settlement total, but only if the net amount to our clients is acceptable to them. There are some companies that won't offer our full fees for an out of court repurchase settlement in which case the remaining balance comes out from the refund portion of the settlement, but we negotiate the mileage fee as low as possible to offset that so our clients still usually do better than or at least equivalent to what they could get if they won in court.

Many lemon law firms talk a big game and claim there is no out of pocket charge for Lemon Law representation, but when you sign up with them, there are all kinds of ways you can be charged out-of-pocket for the representation and because they have no fair fee guarantee the fee the attorney gets out of settlement could be more than what you get. We don't do that.

One of the most common complaints we hear from clients about other law firms is how difficult it is to get their attorneys on the phone. We do the opposite and pride ourselves on our accessibility to clients. Here's how…

We have a firm policy of taking client calls immediately as long as we're not handling another matter. If we're unavailable when you call, we return all calls within one business day. We also email clients for convenience but always call with important developments. These policies ensure we're easily accessible to our clients.

INDEX

NOTES

Made in the USA
Monee, IL
05 November 2026

67387968R00050